Mother
Nature's
vacuum
cleaner.

The world's most

atrocious*

~~fearsome~~

animals.

*or are they?

happy yak

For Oliver & Nathan.
P.B.

Croc ← connoisseurs.

↑
A bit snappy,
to say the least.

Not so
itsy bitsy.
↓

© 2023 Quarto Publishing Group USA Inc.
Text and illustration: © 2023 Philip Bunting
Original series concept by: Rhiannon Findlay

Philip Bunting has asserted his right to be identified
as the author and illustrator of this work.

Designers: Philip Bunting & Sarah Chapman-Suire
Commissioning Editor: Carly Madden
Editor: Nancy Dickmann
Consultant: Michael Bright
Creative Director: Malena Stojić
Associate Publisher: Rhiannon Findlay

First published in 2023 by Happy Yak, an imprint of The Quarto Group.
100 Cummings Center, Suite 265D, Beverly, MA 01915, USA.
T (978)282-9590 F (978)283-2742
www.quarto.com

A CIP record for this book is available from the Library of Congress.

ISBN 978 0 7112 8367 1
eBook ISBN 978 0 7112 8725 9

Manufactured in Guangdong, China TT112023
9 8 7 6 5 4 3 2

Contents.

A real monster.
↓

Wild sense of → humor.

No ray of sunshine.
↓

Introduction.

Whether by tooth or claw, size or stealth, brains or brawn, each of the creatures in the following pages has earned a pretty fearsome reputation. But do they really deserve it? The animals we fear the most are not always the biggest—scary creatures can come in all shapes and sizes. They can be sneaky, creepy, and sometimes simply nasty, brutish, and short. But there are all sorts of reasons why these beasts send shivers down our spines.

Fear can come in the form of ~~bats~~ blood-suckers (p64)... ~~reptiles~~ dragons (p15)...yikes!...and ~~lizards~~ monsters (p60). Hey, please stop that! Sometimes, our fear comes from the things we can't see (but we know are there...and also happen to have hundreds of massive teeth). Let's meet a few of the world's most ~~fearsome~~ atrocious animals. Are you going to do this all the way through?

Grizzly bear.

~~Ursus arctos horribilis.~~
Grizzlius maximus.

Will eat
other bears:
grizzly, black,
brown, and
gummy.

Hibernates
for 5-7 months
every year.
(Do not wake.)

Humpback
(the hump is a
massive muscle).
Argh!

Can eat
up to 90 lb
per day!

Young ones
can climb
trees!
There goes
that escape
plan...

Super
salmon
snatchers.

These terrifying creatures are the top predator in their North American home.
Averaging around 6.5 ft long (with larger males weighing up to 800 lb), they
can hunt huge herbivores such as bison and moose (but also have a soft spot
for salmon and blueberries). Their claws are about as long as an adult human's
fingers and they can run at up to 35 mi per hour (much faster than even the
quickest human). You have been warned!

Deathstalker scorpion.

~~Leiurus quinquestriatus.~~

Lethalus landlobsterus.

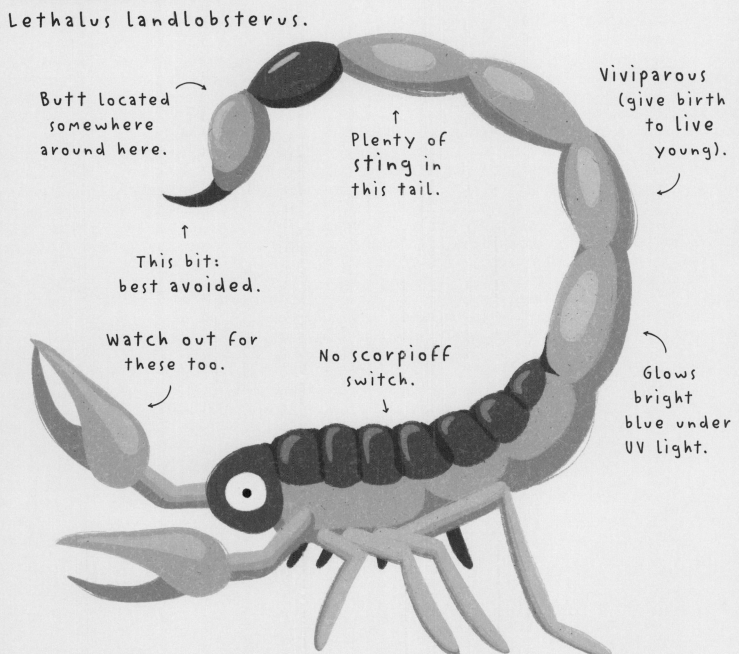

Butt located somewhere around here.

↑ Plenty of sting in this tail.

Viviparous (give birth to live young).

↑ This bit: best avoided.

Watch out for these too.

No scorpioff switch. ↓

Glows bright blue under UV light.

Scorpions are a part of the arachnid family—along with spiders—so they are not insects. Fossils suggest that ancient scorpions were one of the first sea creatures to crawl onto dry land, around 420 million years ago. Today, there are around 1,500 species in this fearsome family, with the deathstalker considered one of the most aggressive and deadly. It lives in North Africa and the Middle East, and its potent venom is a cocktail of neurotoxins, which can cause extreme pain and anaphylaxis (a life-threatening allergic reaction) to anyone unlucky enough to get stung.

Leopard seal.

~~Hydrurga leptonyx.~~

Polkadotus atrocious.

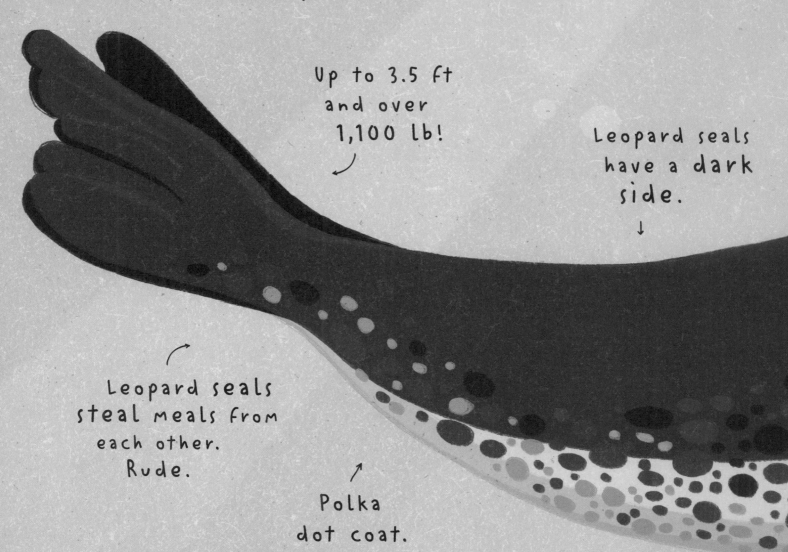

Up to 3.5 ft and over 1,100 lb!

Leopard seals have a dark side. ↓

Leopard seals steal meals from each other. Rude.

Polka dot coat. Fancy.

These cold-water carnivores could never be described as picky eaters—fish, squid, seabirds, other seals, sharks, and crustaceans are all on the menu for leopard seals. But thanks to a set of sievelike cheek teeth, their Southern Ocean diet consists mainly of krill (tiny shrimplike crustaceans), which leopard seals slurp down in vast quantities. Because of their size (reaching up to 11.5 ft in length), leopard seals are at the top of the food chain in the Antarctic—their only known predator being orcas.

Can't wear sunglasses.

No earflaps (unlike sea lions).

Plays with its food.
↓

Poor ol' penguins. Snack food of the Southern Ocean.
↓

Jaws can open up to 160°!

160°

Seafood diet: See food, eat food.

Leopard seals can reach speeds of up to 23 mi per hour, quick enough to leap out of the water and onto an ice floe. They can stay submerged for around 15 minutes while hunting, and are even known to sing to one another while underwater. But don't be fooled by those siren songs—leopard seals have a dark side, too. Once they've eaten enough food for the day, these massive mammals will often chase smaller creatures for fun, giving them a reputation as bullies.

Red-bellied piranha.

~~Pygocentrus nattereri.~~

Chompus chompus.

Aquarium pet
for all good
supervillains.

Gill-ty
expression.

Toothy
terror.

Do not
pet!

Nightmarish
gnashers.

There are no
registered dentists
in Piranhaland
(not anymore).

Despite their fearsome reputation, these South American freshwater fish typically scavenge for food rather than hunt it. As a relatively social species, they swim in shoals for safety but are also known to grunt, gnash, and "bark" while communicating with one another! And while it goes without saying that these toothy terrors can pack quite a bite, piranha attacks on unlucky humans are very rare.

Common hippopotamus.

~~Hippopotamus amphibius.~~

Hangreus chargeus.

Hangry
Hangry
← Hippo.

Stole Shrek's →
ears.

← Say "aah."
Argh!

A group of
hippos is called
a bloat.

Communicate
through poop!
Perhaps a more
appropriate
name might be
hippobottomus.

Terrible →
swimmer.

Our planet's second-largest land animal weighs as much as three cars and can (and will) gallop toward you at up to 19 mi per hour! A hippo's most terrifying feature is its enormous jaws. Hippos can open their mouths to almost 180°, exposing their colossal canines before chomping down with one of the strongest bite forces in the animal kingdom. Scarier still, hippos are known to be omnivorous, meaning they are not averse to the odd meaty meal.

Green anaconda.

Sssquashus
sssqueezus.

Anacondas can
find it hard
to unwind.

These colossal carnivores belong to a family called
constrictors. Green anacondas will eat pretty
much anything they can wrap their jaws around—from
caimans to capybaras—and prefer to do their hunting at
night. Once it catches its prey, a green anaconda will wrap
its powerful body around the victim, before slowly squeezing
it to death. Once the creature has stopped squirming, the
green anaconda will quite literally swallow it whole.

Ssseriously
big sssnake.
↓

← 8.5 m →

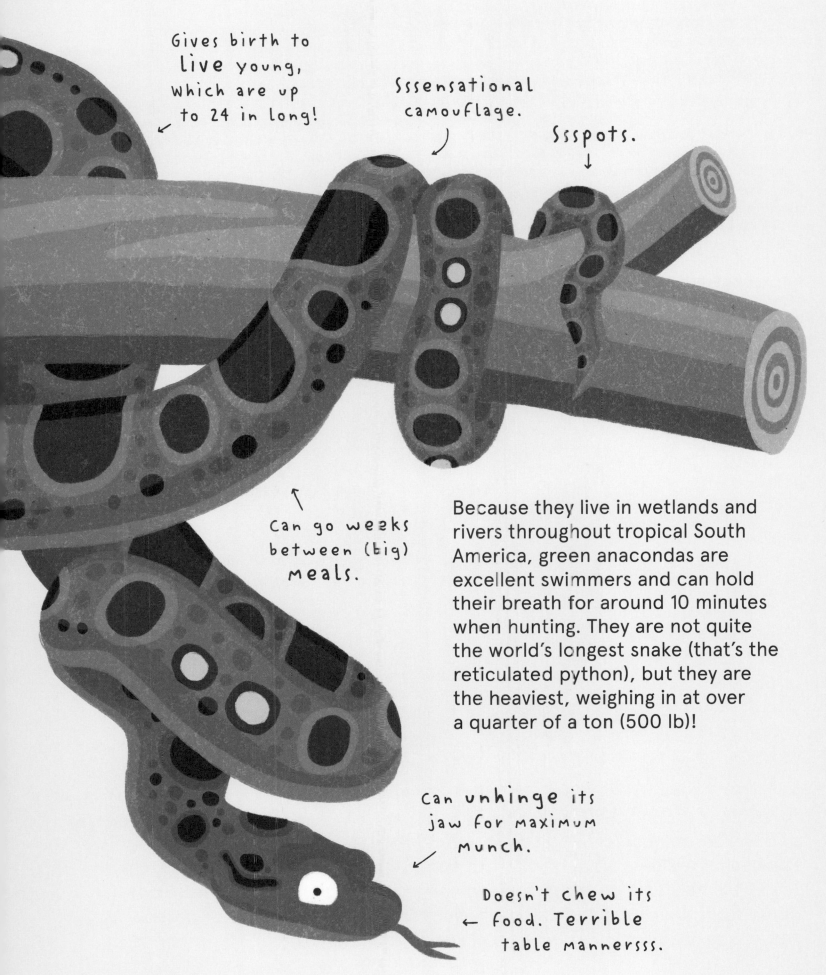

Gives birth to **live** young, which are up to 24 in long!

Sssensational camouflage.

Ssspots.

Can go weeks between (big) **meals**.

Because they live in wetlands and rivers throughout tropical South America, green anacondas are excellent swimmers and can hold their breath for around 10 minutes when hunting. They are not quite the world's longest snake (that's the reticulated python), but they are the heaviest, weighing in at over a quarter of a ton (500 lb)!

Can unhinge its jaw for maximum munch.

Doesn't chew its food. Terrible table mannersss.

Tasmanian devil.

~~Sarcophilus harrisii.~~

Screecheus growlii.

A bit of a scavenger.

Mother Nature's vacuum cleaner.

Stinky breath. Pee-ew!

Bone-crunching → jaws.

← Bloodcurdling scream.

Favorite pastime? Carrion Chomping.

Chubby tail stores fat.

Screeching around their Australian island home of Tasmania, the world's largest carnivorous marsupial weighs in at around the size of a small dog. Tassie devils have an incredibly strong bite, which comes in handy when tucking into their favorite meal—carrion (already-dead animals). But their devilish name doesn't come from their terrible table manners—it's from the selection of creepy calls they make, including growls, snorts, screeches, and yelps!

Komodo dragon.

~~Varanus komodoensis.~~

Venom-nom-nomus horriblis.

Terrible parent. ↓

Can't fly... or breathe fire.

Bony skin.

Always dragon their feet. ↓

↑ Can smell you from 7.5 mi away.

Found only on a few Indonesian islands, these 8.5-ft monsters are one of only a few venomous lizards on the planet. When a Komodo bites its prey, its venom seeps into the wound. If the animal escapes the initial attack, the dragon will follow it—sometimes for days on end—patiently waiting for the venom to do its thing. If they lose sight of their prey, slow-moving Komodo dragons can use their incredible sense of smell to track it. Known for their appetite, these dragons will not think twice about eating their own offspring.

Colossal squid.

~~Mesonychoteuthis hamiltoni.~~

Calamari colossus.

Eight arms.
Two tentacles.
No two arms
are itentical.

↑
Came from
another planet!
Just squidding.

When they let rip,
it really inks.

Invertebrates are animals with no backbone, and the largest type can weigh up to 1,650 lb and stretch up to 48 ft long (but probably longer). The colossal squid has the largest eyes of any animal—with each one growing beyond the size of a soccer ball (10 in)! Little is known about these secretive cephalopods, as they so rarely come into contact with humans, thanks to their vastly deep, dark Antarctic environment.

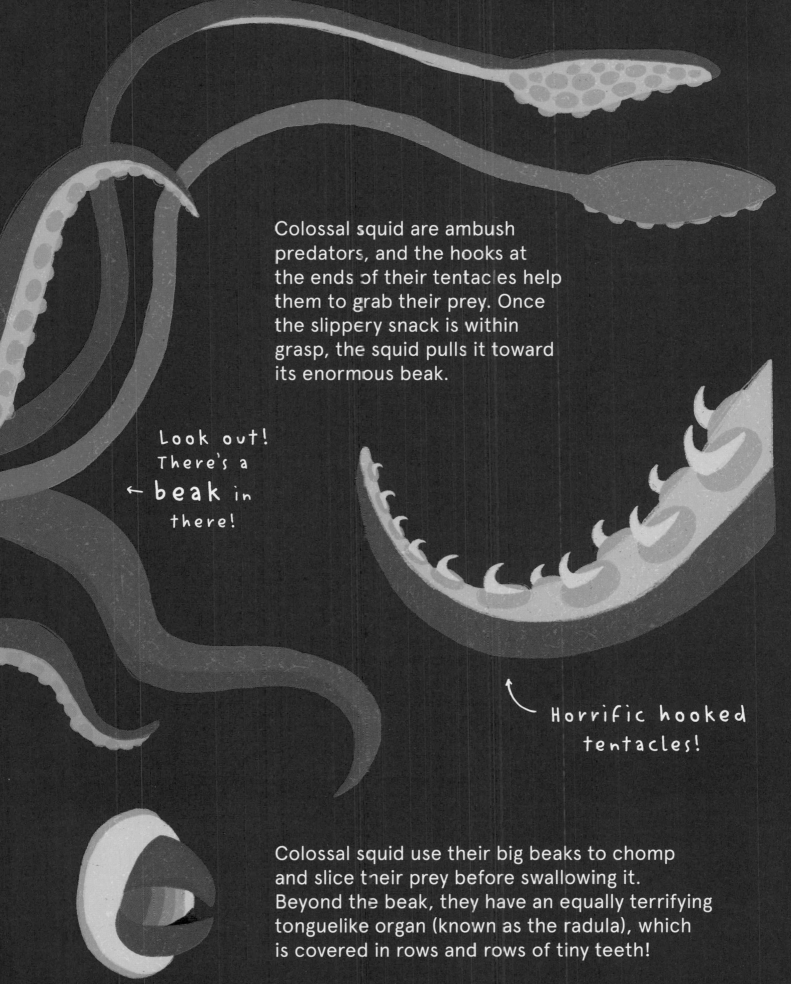

Colossal squid are ambush predators, and the hooks at the ends of their tentacles help them to grab their prey. Once the slippery snack is within grasp, the squid pulls it toward its enormous beak.

Look out! There's a
← **beak** in there!

Horrific hooked tentacles!

Colossal squid use their big beaks to chomp and slice their prey before swallowing it. Beyond the beak, they have an equally terrifying tonguelike organ (known as the radula), which is covered in rows and rows of tiny teeth!

Crowned eagle.

~~Stephanoaetus coronatus.~~

Regalus eaglus.

Lock up your babies! ↓

A real royal → terror.

The crown is a bit pretentious. ↘

Massive → monkey-snatchers.

No Prince Charming. ↖

Crowned eagles are probably the most powerful of the African eagles. Their favorite food is primates, especially the monkeys that live in their sub-Saharan home. There are even tales of these hair-raising raptors also hunting small children. Yikes! Beyond us hairy humans, crowned eagles will also go for mongooses, cats, rats, lizards, and even antelope—they are known to take prey up to six times their own weight, thanks to their incredibly powerful legs, and huge hooked talons, which can reach 2.5 in long.

Geography cone snail.

~~Conus geographus.~~

Slowus pokeus.

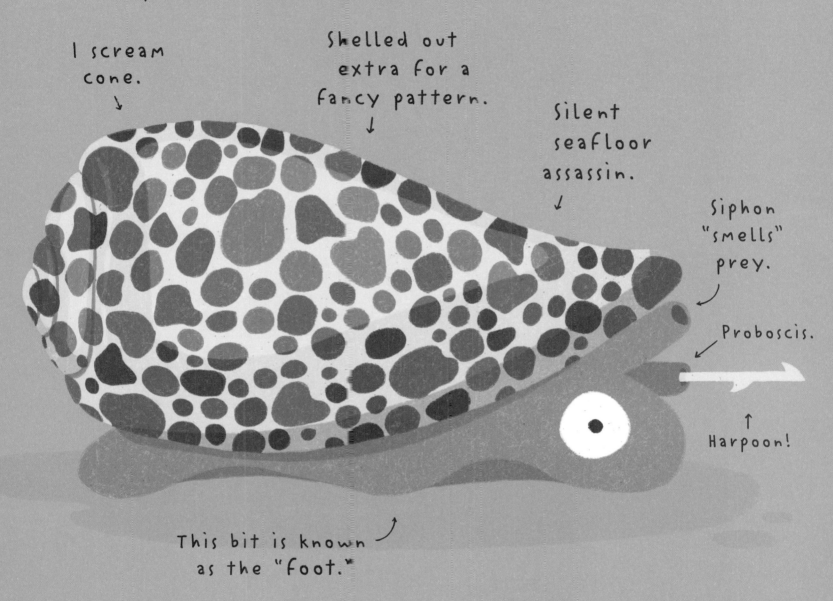

I scream cone.

Shelled out extra for a fancy pattern.

Silent seafloor assassin.

Siphon "smells" prey.

Proboscis.

↑ Harpoon!

This bit is known as the "foot."

These predatory molluscs come packing their own harpoon, with a venom more than capable of finishing off an adult human. Cone snails are relatively small (4-6 in) and slow-moving (it's not called a snail's pace for nothing), so they rely on their special weapon to hunt and defend themselves. The harpoonlike tooth can be pushed out at over 370 mi per hour to inject toxins into their prey, before the snail sucks up its victim whole. There are around 500 known species of cone snail, but the geography cone is thought to pack the deadliest punch (and swimmers be warned...there is no known antivenom).

Amazonian giant centipede.

~~Scolopendra gigantea.~~

Bezosium horrificus.

Growing up to 12 in (and most likely even longer), these carnivorous, venomous woodland giants will munch any meat they can get their mandibles on (including your little finger)! As they scuttle through their South American home, these super-quick, nocturnal hunters attack with a venom that's potent enough to take down most insects, amphibians, and mammals. Their venom is injected through the centipede's forcipules (those red stingerlike "legs" near the head).

Do not try this at → home, kids!

Eeek!
↙

Argh!
↓

Yikes!
↓

Estuarine stonefish.

~~Synanceia horrida.~~

Gargoyleus ouchea.

The most toxic fish in the world!

Mother Nature's deadliest Lego brick.

Is it a stone?
Is it a fish?
No, it's...
Oooooouch!

Nothing to see here.

Not a stepping stone.

Stonefish are so well camouflaged that they are often mistaken for, well, stones, and subsequently stepped on. This causes the downtrodden stonefish to push venom through the sharp spines on its back, and into the foot of the unfortunate wader. While stonefish only use their venom as a defense mechanism, they are one of the deadliest animals in Australia (a country with more than its fair share of dangerous critters), and the most venomous fish in the world. So think twice before you step on a stone down under.

Giant spitting cobra.

~~Naja ashei.~~

Sniperus venomous.

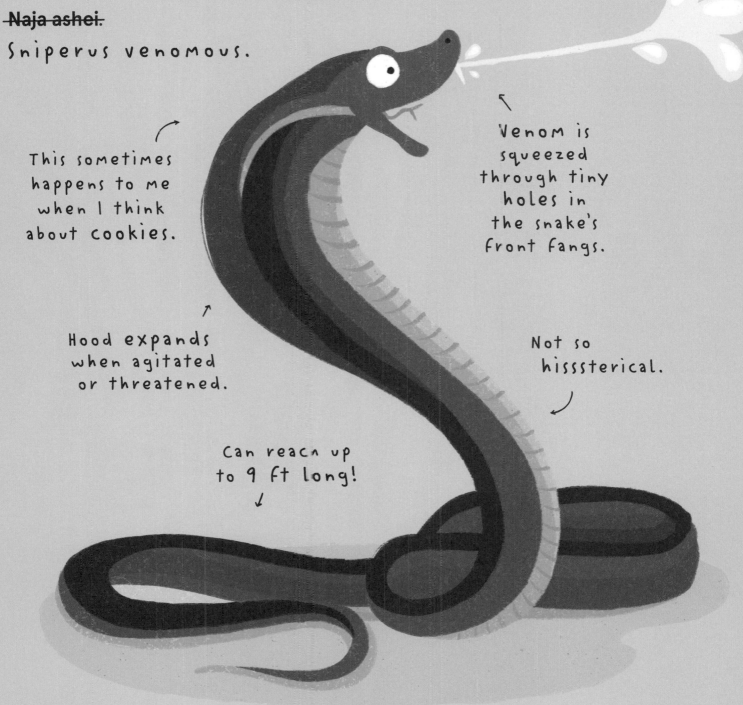

This sometimes happens to me when I think about cookies.

Venom is squeezed through tiny holes in the snake's front fangs.

Hood expands when agitated or threatened.

Not so hisssterical.

Can reach up to 9 ft long!

When these colossal cobras feel threatened, they squirt a cocktail of toxic venom so potent that it can break down the flesh of their assailant. Worse still, the venom is generally directed at the eyes of the attacker (or innocent bystander, in some cases). If not washed away very quickly, the cobra's venom can quickly cause severe pain and even lead to blindness. These superpowered snakes use this ability as a defense mechanism, rather than for hunting. You have been warned!

Siberian tiger.

~~Panthera tigris tigris.~~ ↑
The i
of the
tiger.

Fur-ocious
felinius.

Their coats are →
like snowflakes
or fingerprints—
no two are
identical.

Tip: don't ↗
call it a
snowflake.

Of the nine subspecies of tiger in the world, the Siberian tiger is the largest, which makes it the biggest cat on Earth. Also known as Amur tigers, these stripy assassins can grow over 11 ft long and weigh over 880 lb (around the weight of five adult humans!). Because they live in cold eastern Russia, their bodies are insulated by thick layers of fat and fur, like a built-in snowsuit.

Built-in
night-vision
goggles.
↓

↑
Canines can
grow over
5 in long!

↑
Can jump up to
16.5 ft in the air!

↰
Webbed toes
to swim faster.

These Siberian superpredators travel huge distances in search of food, and hunt by stealth—sneaking up on their prey before pouncing. While they will snack on smaller animals such as rabbits, birds, and fish, Siberian tigers prefer a heartier meal and will seek out large mammals such as wild boar, deer, elk, and even bears!

Tapeworm.

~~Taenia.~~

Ribbonae
rascalii.

May be in your
guts right now.
↓

Eew. ↗

Eew.
↓

Eew.
↓

Eew.
↑

↖ So gross.

Can control
minds. ↘

Eew.
↓

~~Tapeworms
are the best.~~
↓

Argh! My tapeworm
told me to say that!

Tapeworms are ancient parasites that live in the intestines of other animals
(you and me included). Their heads are equipped with hooks and suction
cups to hold on to the digestive tracts of their hosts. These ribbonlike
rascals range in length from a fraction of an inch up to almost 130 ft!
Fossilized tapeworm eggs have been found in the prehistoric poop of a
270-million-year-old shark. While they may appear primitive, some species
of tapeworm are able to control the minds—and therefore the behavior—of
their hosts, including ants, stickleback fish, and snails.

Gray wolf.

~~Canis lupus.~~

Biggus Baddus.

Can smell 100 times better than you.

Do not wolf whistle.

All the better to sniff you with.

Hairy legs.

Always wolfs down its food. Rude.

If your grandmother looks like this...run!

The gray wolf is the original ancestor of all domestic dogs. Yep, even pugs. These predators tend to live in small family groups called packs. A pack is led by a mother and father wolf, who teach their offspring to work together to bring down huge animals, such as reindeer and moose. Wolves rely on their incredible intellect and communication skills to hunt. Their famous howl can be heard from over 9 mi away, and can be used to help defend territory, warn of danger, and even find missing pack members. Gray wolves help control the number of herbivores in their environment, helping to maintain the natural balance of their native ecosystems.

Orca.

~~Orcinus orca.~~

Dolphinii notsofriendlius.

↑
They do not chew—can swallow seals whole. Gulp!

↖
No need for an orcadontist.

They sing together to form an orcastra.

Also known as killer whales, orcas are the largest member of the dolphin family, reaching up to 26 ft in length and weighing up to 11,000 lb! These top predators can be found in every ocean on Earth, making them the most widespread mammal in the world, after humans. And just like us, orcas are incredibly social creatures, living and hunting together in pods of up to 40. Orcas in different parts of the world communicate with different languages and have developed their own diets and behaviors.

28

Just eat me.

Orcas play with their food. We're not sure why.

Orcas are prolific predators and will hunt by themselves or in pods to keep their bellies full, with an adult eating well over 440 lb of creatures per day! Their diet is wide and depends upon where they live, but orcas will eat fish, sea lions and seals, sharks, turtles, penguins, squid, octopus, and even other dolphins and whales. Orca pods have been known to join together to hunt larger animals— even blue whales!

No sense of smell (or mercy).

Killer ~~whale~~ dolphin.

Blue-ringed octopus.

~~Hapalochlaena lunulata.~~

Flashus bitus.

No known antivenom. ↙

Blue rings pulsate before an attack! ↘

Rascal of the rockpool. ↙

What a show-off. →

Blue-ringed bully. ↙

One of the most venomous animals in the world is surprisingly tiny. The "head" of the blue-ringed octopus is only about the size of a golf ball, while the whole creature measures just 8 in long. But what they lack in size, they make up for in venom. Each individual has enough venom to knock off around 25 adult humans within minutes! Worse still, the blue-ringed octopus is incredibly aggressive, and will often pick a fight, rather than flee danger. They bite prey to inject venom, and sometimes also release a cloud of venom into the water, then wait for unsuspecting fish and crustaceans to pass through.

Chimpanzee.

~~Pan troglodytes.~~

Almostus likeus.

Make tools (such as spears) to hunt with!

The genetic difference between you and this guy → is mostly fur, teeth, and a taste for monkeys.

Do not invite → them to your tea party.

That banana skin just winked at me.

Monkey muncher.

Chimps go to war with rival bands.

We share over 98 percent of our genes with chimps! We also share more than 60 percent of our genetic material with bananas, so that 2 percent difference is more significant than it sounds. Our super-smart cousins live in socially ordered communities and communicate with one another through highly complex sounds, gestures, and facial expressions (just like us). And like humans, chimps are an omnivorous species, which means they will eat just about anything. But perhaps more atrociously, they will even eat other primates. Chimps prefer the savory flavors of red colobus monkeys to bananas.

Northern giant hornet.

~~Vespa mandarinia.~~

Humongous horriblis.

Butcher of bees.

Can fly 60 mi per day.

Flesh-melting → venom.

Also known as the murder hornet, these thumb-sized mega-wasps are some of the most venomous insects on the planet. The hornet's ¼ in stinger injects a horrible venom, which both destroys tissue and shuts down the nervous system of its victims. These aggressive, predatory insects hunt a variety of bugs, targeting those much larger than themselves, such as the praying mantis. Worse still, Asian northern giant hornets are known to attack in swarms! While a single sting is incredibly painful, it is typically not fatal to humans... however, multiple stings from a swarm of these humongous hornets most certainly can be.

While they might seem terrifying to us, the creature most terrorized by the murder hornet is the honeybee. The horrible hornets commonly work together to ransack entire beehives, stealing the honey and honeybee larvae for their lunch. The hornets use their massive mandibles to snip the heads of the bees clean off, then carry the larvae back to their nests, to feed their own babies.

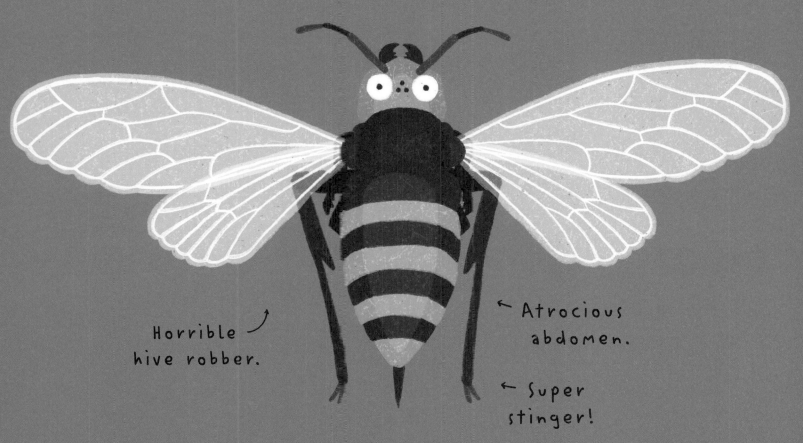

African bush elephant.

~~Loxodonta africana.~~

Stompus grumpus.

If there really is an elephant in the room...run!

Adults eat around 330 lb of food per day (roughly 375 cans of beans). Greedy.

Super-sensitive schnoz.

Terrible tusks (actually massive incisor teeth).

Musth dash. →

The largest land mammals in the world live in herds mainly made up of related females and young males, with older males preferring to go it alone. While elephants are typically intelligent and gentle creatures, adult males go through a period called musth, when they become a little less gentle. Males in musth become very energetic, irritable, aggressive, and generally quite dangerous for up to 3 months. While we're not quite sure why male elephants go through musth, it is thought to be related to social signals and mating.

Hooded pitohui.

~~Pitohui dichrous.~~

Robin deathbreast.

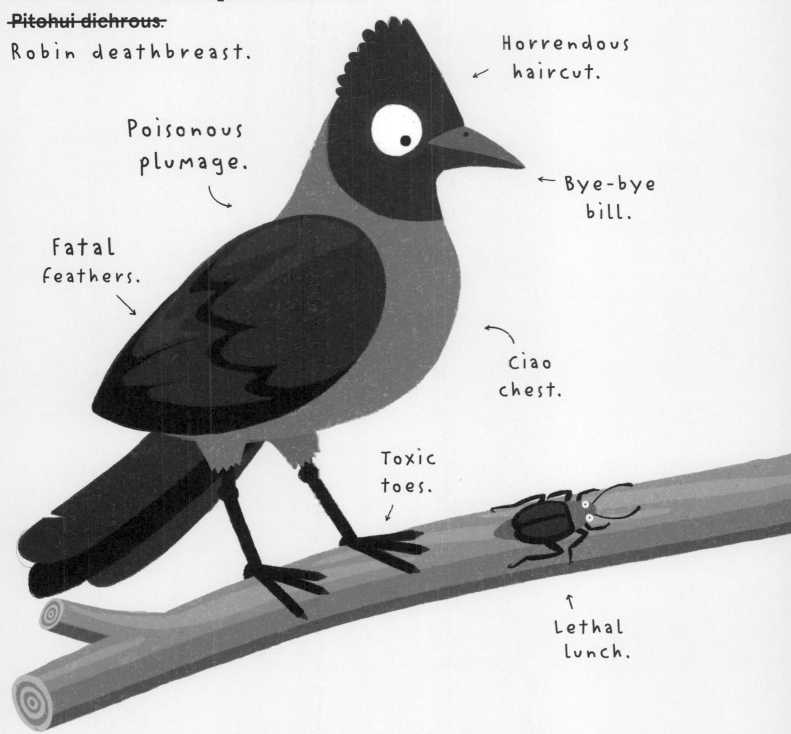

Poisonous plumage.

Horrendous haircut.

Bye-bye bill.

Fatal feathers.

Ciao chest.

Toxic toes.

Lethal lunch.

Believed to be the world's most poisonous bird, hooded pitohui are a common sight throughout their island home of New Guinea. These bold birds pack poison in their feathers and skin that is toxic enough to put off most predators, and cause the local human population to name them pitohui (which means "rubbish bird"!). They don't make their poison themselves, but get it directly from the food they eat—such as the toxin-filled Choresine beetles.

Saltwater crocodile.

~~Crocodylus porosus.~~

Saltius maximus.

Can hold
their breath
for an hour.
↓

Don't be taken in
by the grin. They're
quite salty, really.
↓

Always on! Crocs sleep
with one eye open,
and one half of their
brain still awake!

If a tooth is lost, another
one will soon grow back.
A tooth fairy's dream.

Stubby legs aren't →
too quick on land.

The largest reptiles in the world can reach up to 23 ft in length, and up to 2,200 lb in weight. The crocodile family has been around for a long time—they first appeared over 250 million years ago, and haven't found the need to change too much since then. In their time, crocs have dined on dinosaurs and skated through the Ice Age, all the while maintaining their spot at the top of the food chain. Now perfectly adapted to life as an ambush predator, salties are aggressive and incredibly dangerous—especially in the water.

Tend to
be a bit
snappy.
↓

Swallow stones
to help digest
food.
↓

Stomach acid capable
of digesting bones,
beaks, horns, hooves,
shells, your dad's
cooking...
↓

Their long, lumpy bodies and powerful tails are perfectly adapted to allow
saltwater crocs to swim underwater without even causing a ripple on the
surface. When submerged, they can reach speeds of up to 20 mi per hour as
they propel themselves toward their land-loving prey at the edge of the water.
When they launch an attack, salties can lunge an entire body-length out of the
water to snap up a snack. Their jaws are powerful enough to chomp through
large mammal bones, before pulling their prey underwater to finish it off.

Honey badger.

~~Mellivora capensis.~~

Stinkbombus ferocious.

Teeth can break through a tortoise shell!

Not really a badger (more of a solitary weasel).

Thick, rubbery skin helps in a fight.

Super stinky gland to mark territory and release stink bombs!

Yikes!

Don't be fooled by the name! These burly badgers are anything but sweet. When faced with a foe—whether that be a lion, hyena, leopard, snake, or wild dog—the super-aggressive honey badger produces a display of defiance that would send any potential predator back to where it came from. Puffing out its hair until it stands on end, the badger will release a stink bomb, then scream with a bloodcurdling roar, before charging tooth and claw at its enemy!

Hawaiian carnivorous caterpillar.

~~Eupithecia orichloris.~~

Veryhungreous carnivorous.

While a little green caterpillar might not seem too fearsome to you and me, in its world, this creature is a monster. Hawaiian carnivorous caterpillars are the larval (juvenile) stage of a group of moths native to Hawaii. While most other caterpillars are happy munching their way through leaves, these proto-moths have evolved a taste for bugs. Anchoring their hind legs to a branch or leaf, these super-stealthy ambush hunters wait patiently for a passing bug. Once the lunch-to-be touches one of their super-sensitive setae (hair-like bristles), they strike out, grasping the prey with claws that stab through the victim's tough exoskeleton.

Lunch.
↓

Needle-like claws.

Eats vegetarian caterpillars for breakfast.
↓

Strikes in a fraction of a second.

Not a fan of pineapples (on pizza or otherwise).

Alligator snapping turtle.

~~Macrochelys temminckii.~~

Shellus chompus.

Can live up to 150 years!

Not a picky eater. ↓

Ooh, yum.

↑
Will eat human fingers if pushed.

These frisky freshwater turtles are native to the United States and can weigh in at up to 175 lb (around the same as an adult human). Their mighty bite is powerful enough to chomp through bones. Alligator snapping turtles will eat most fish, amphibians, molluscs, birds, worms, crustaceans, small mammals...and more. They have even been known to attack and eat young alligators!

Alligator snapping turtles are top predators in the Mississippi River system. They help control the populations of their prey, and in doing so help maintain the natural order of their ecosystem.

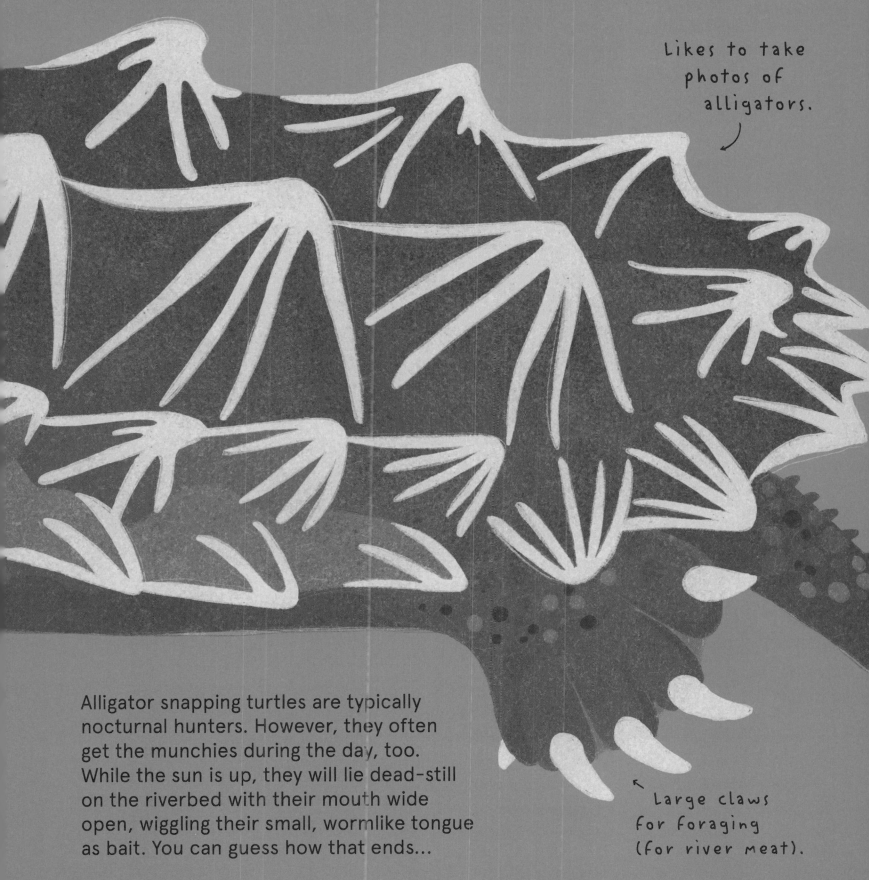

Likes to take photos of alligators.

Alligator snapping turtles are typically nocturnal hunters. However, they often get the munchies during the day, too. While the sun is up, they will lie dead-still on the riverbed with their mouth wide open, wiggling their small, wormlike tongue as bait. You can guess how that ends...

Large claws for foraging (for river meat).

Atlantic wolffish.

 ~~Anarhichas lupus.~~

Antifreezus
toothiface.

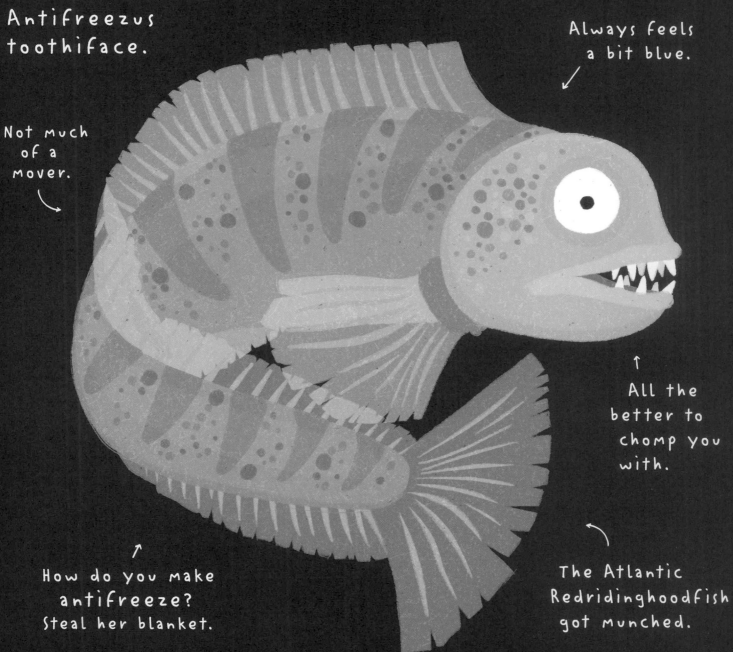

Always feels
a bit blue.

Not much
of a
mover.

All the
better to
chomp you
with.

How do you make
antifreeze?
Steal her blanket.

The Atlantic
Redridinghoodfish
got munched.

These solitary coldwater fish grow to around 5 ft long, and are also called things like devilfish, seawolf, leopardfish, or wolf eel. These names come from their fanglike teeth, which are perfectly evolved for cracking through the shells of crabs, mussels, and urchins. Wolffish mostly stay in rocky nooks on the seafloor. They can live in the Arctic Circle and to help combat the cold, they have evolved antifreeze properties in their blood, to help keep things pumping.

Redback spider.

~~Latrodectus hasselti.~~

Mateus munchus.

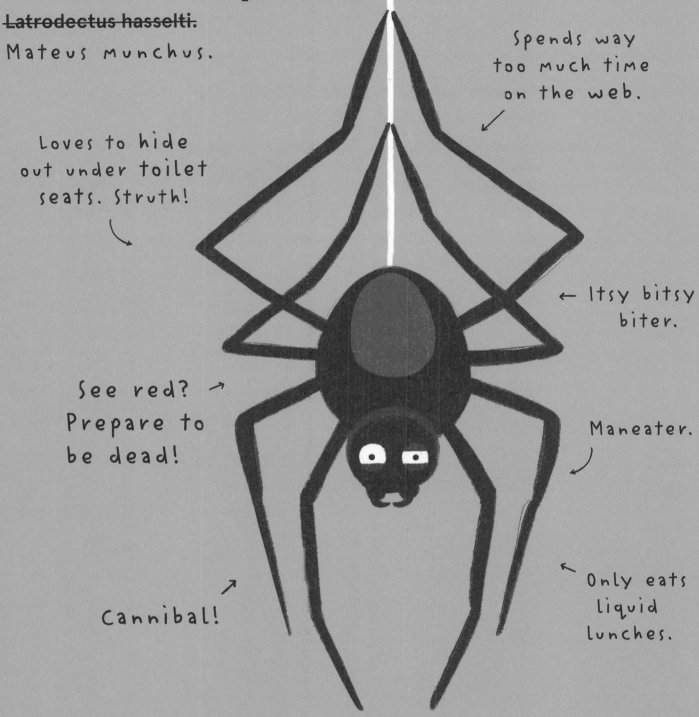

Loves to hide out under toilet seats. Struth!

Spends way too much time on the web.

See red? Prepare to be dead!

← Itsy bitsy biter.

Maneater.

Cannibal!

← Only eats liquid lunches.

While typically less than ½ in long, female redbacks can weigh up to 100 times more than their miniscule mates. Worse still for the boys, female redbacks have a rather nasty habit of eating the male after mating! We humans fare a little better—but not much—with redback bites being the most common venomous spider bites in Australia. They pack a poison that can affect our nerve cells. Redbacks typically use it to paralyze small prey, before liquefying and sucking out their insides.

Regal horned lizard.

~~Phrynosoma solare.~~

Bloodius squirtii.

These royally named reptiles were given their title thanks
to the crownlike array of horns around their head.
But their behavior can be anything but regal. Thanks to
millions of years of adaptation—specifically adapting
to not being munched—regal horned lizards have
evolved a very special, very gory means of escaping
predators...the ability to shoot their own blood into
the face of any would-be attacker!

Eew.
↓

Crown of
horns.

Inflatable
escape
artist.
↓

Scaly sharp
shooter.
↓

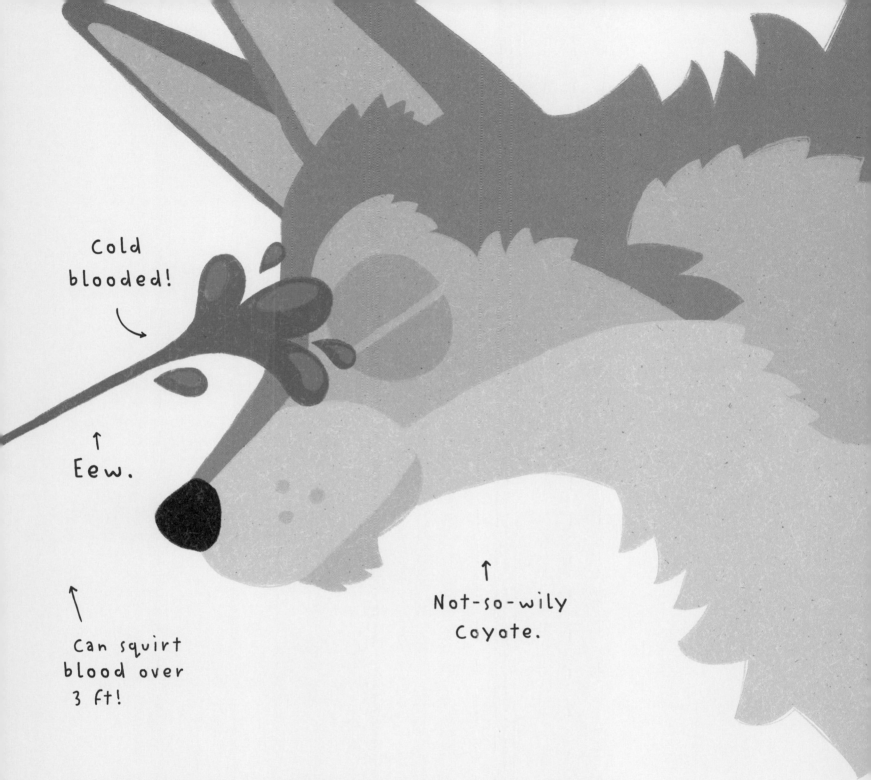

Cold blooded!

Eew.

Can squirt blood over 3 ft!

Not-so-wily Coyote.

This surprising spray is triggered by the lizard as a last resort, when face-to-face with a predator such as a coyote, roadrunner, or rattlesnake. Regal horned lizards burst a blood vessel in the skin beneath their eyeballs to launch their stream of gory gloop. As the predator reels in shock, the lizard makes its escape. And just in case the bloody super-soaker isn't enough, regal horned lizards have one more defensive trick up their scaly sleeves—the ability to suck in air and blow up like a balloon, making them appear too massive to munch!

Loggerhead shrike.

~~Lanius ludovicianus.~~

Spikesis luncheous.

Loves a lubber lollypop.

A group of shrikes is called an abattoir.

Shrike. →
Shriek!

Sun-dried grasshopper. Method: 2 days at 77°F.

↑
Shrikes may use a row of such "treats" to attract a mate.

Shrikes are medium-sized predatory songbirds who eat mice, lizards, large insects, and even small birds. Also known as butcherbirds, loggerheads impale their prey on thorns and even barbed-wire fences, storing their food for later in little "larders." North American loggerhead shrikes particularly enjoy snacking on a toxin-filled insect known as the lubber grasshopper. When a shrike catches an unlucky lubber, the bird impales it and leaves it for at least a couple of days before eating it. This way the toxins in the grasshopper will have broken down, and are no longer a threat to the bird.

Red kangaroo.

~~Macropus rufus.~~

Biggus reddus.

Monstrous marsupial (the biggest on Earth).

Don't call him → "Skippy."

Can jump 6 ft high and over a distance of 29 ft!

← Hopping mad.

Fearsome flesh-ripping claws.

← Cannot moonwalk. (Roos cannot walk backward.)

The largest species of kangaroo, big reds can stand at over 6.5 ft tall and weigh over 200 lb. These super-heavyweight marsupials box each other to compete for territory and mates. When they see red, these big roos can kick out with over 2,000 lb of force! Known to attack humans who get a little too familiar, red kangaroos will grab their target with their forepaws, and kick with their hind legs, raking down the body with huge toe claws. Yowza.

African giant swallowtail.

~~Papilio antimachus.~~
Papilio poisono.

Anti-social
butterfly.
↓

Monarch of
mischief.
↓

Indigestible
insect.

Will give you →
much more than
butterflies in
your tummy.

With a wingspan of up to 9 in, the African giant swallowtail is one of the largest butterflies on Earth. It has no natural enemies, thanks to the incredible volume of toxins flowing through its body. It is suspected that the giant swallowtail gains these toxins while still in its larva (caterpillar) form. As grubs, these creatures munch their way through a whole lot of extremely toxic vine leaves. The poisons in these leaves have long been used by people in Somalia to help them hunt. Arrowheads dipped in the toxin are said to be potent enough to bring down a hippo!

Whopping wings!

Brave/silly human.

Fossa.

~~Cryptoprocta ferox.~~ ← Scientific name means "ferocious hidden anus." Ha-ha.

Hilarious namus.

How rude.

Supermongoose masquerading as a big cat.

Lemur's least favorite thing.

Ferocious hidden anus (not pictured).

Retractable claws.

While the largest predatory mammal on Madagascar looks a lot like a big cat, it actually belongs to a ferocious family descended from mongoose-like creatures that landed on the island around 20 million years ago. Atrociously agile and perfectly adapted for hunting in the trees, fossas can climb down tree trunks headfirst, thanks to their catlike claws and long, slender bodies and tails. Their preferred lunch is lemur, but they will eat most small mammals, fish, lizards, frogs...if it has a heartbeat and lives in Madagascar, they'll eat it.

Common death adder.

~~Acanthophis antarcticus.~~

Leafus alonea.

Time to turn over a new leaf? Maybe pick another leaf... →

Quite literally adds death. ↙

Can give birth to up to 42 live young! ↘

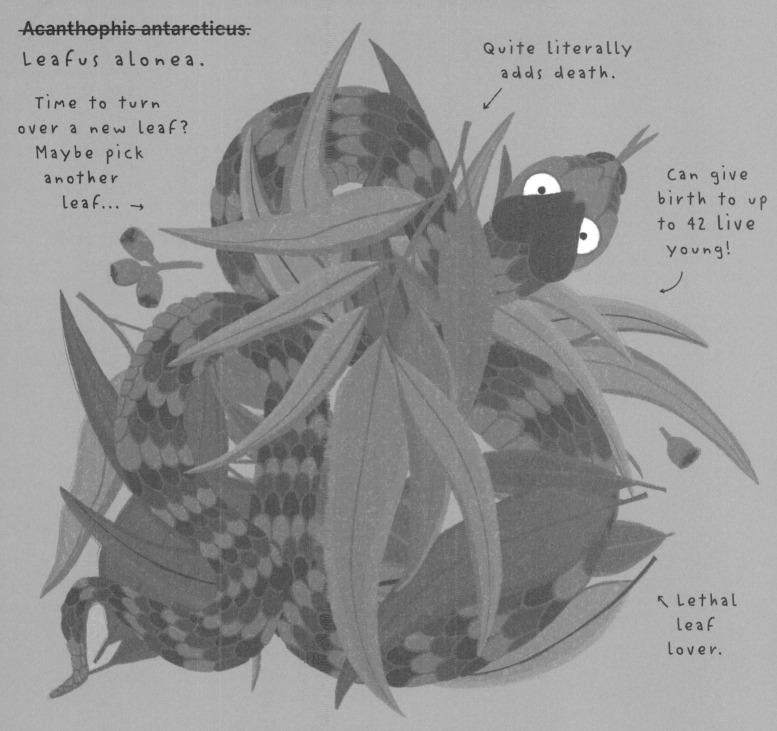

↖ Lethal leaf lover.

Thanks to the solitary, secretive existence of these creatures, most Australians never meet a death adder. These very venomous snakes are typically slow moving and—unlike most snakes—do not pursue their prey. Rather, death adders lie among fallen leaves and wait for lunch to come to them. Once prey is in range, they strike incredibly quickly, injecting a neurotoxin that causes paralysis and death. Before antivenoms were created, roughly 60 percent of death adder attacks on humans were lethal. Hence the name.

Box jellyfish.

~~Cubozoa.~~

Blockus headus.

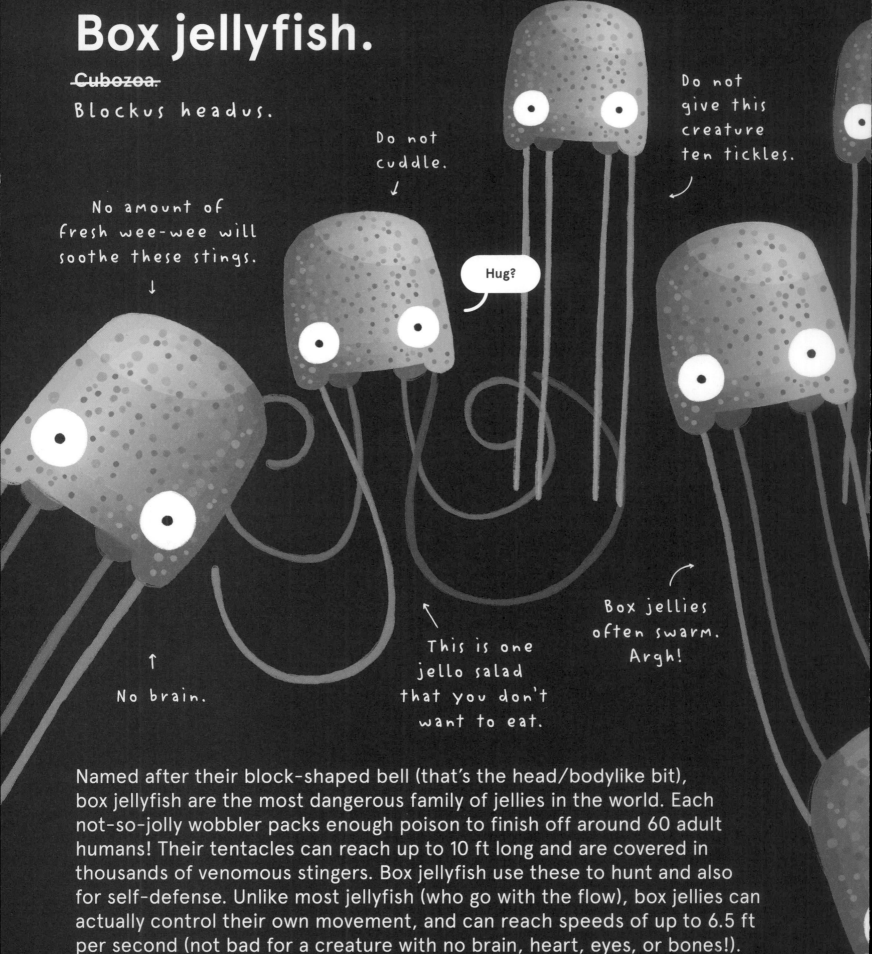

Do not
give this
creature
ten tickles.

Do not
cuddle.
↓

No amount of
fresh wee-wee will
soothe these stings.
↓

Hug?

Box jellies
often swarm.
Argh!

This is one
jello salad
that you don't
want to eat.

↑
No brain.

Named after their block-shaped bell (that's the head/bodylike bit),
box jellyfish are the most dangerous family of jellies in the world. Each
not-so-jolly wobbler packs enough poison to finish off around 60 adult
humans! Their tentacles can reach up to 10 ft long and are covered in
thousands of venomous stingers. Box jellyfish use these to hunt and also
for self-defense. Unlike most jellyfish (who go with the flow), box jellies can
actually control their own movement, and can reach speeds of up to 6.5 ft
per second (not bad for a creature with no brain, heart, eyes, or bones!).

I don't think you're ready for this jelly. ↓

Or this one. ↓

53

Brazilian wandering spider.

~~Phoneutria nigriventer.~~

Warningus! Warningus!

← Very clear body language.

No web. No worries. ↘

Known to hide in bunches of bananas! ↓

Females can lay up to 4,000 eggs per brood! ↘

Fangs for the ~~memories~~ nightmares. ↙

These not-so-tiny dancers are one of the most venomous spider species on the planet. Their bite injects a venom quite capable of taking down an adult human. But before it bites, the Brazilian wandering spider will give you fair warning. It will raise its four frontmost legs (which can span up to 7 in) as if to say "back off!"—before launching an attack. But fear not, these South American scuttlers prefer small prey such as insects, other spiders, small reptiles, and mammals. As they don't spin webs, wandering spiders roam the forest floor at night, actively hunting for prey.

Polar bear.

~~Ursus maritimus.~~

Polaris unbearablis.

Sea bear.
See bear?
Run! Bear!

← Super-sensitive
schnoz can smell
you from far
away!

Big fans of
seal (pinnipeds
not the '90s
singer).

Catch seals
with their
bear hands.

Dinner-
plate-sized
paws!

Blubbery
body keeps
them toasty.

Colossal
4-in
claws.

Built-in
snowshoes.

Weighing over a ton and standing over 10 ft tall, Earth's largest land carnivore is perfectly adapted to the icy Arctic lands it calls home. As well as being able to smell their prey from miles away. polar bears can swim incredible distances to hunt, and have been spotted swimming many, many miles from the nearest land or ice floe! Their large paws are perfectly adapted for paddling, and handily convert to super-wide snowshoes while on land.

Bull shark.

~~Carcharhinus leucas.~~

Nom chompsky.

Can reach
speeds of up to
25 mi per hour
(four times faster
than the fastest
human). Gulp.*

Unlike most sharks,
bullies give birth to
live, terrifying
young.

Considered to be the most dangerous sharks in the world, these aggressive, bullish sharks share many of their habitats with us. Bull sharks prefer to eat fish and other sharks. But because they tend to live around rivers and warm, shallow seas (where people like to swim and fish), they're not averse to taking a nibble on the odd knee, or making an appetizer of an ankle.

Bull sharks have evolved to thrive in both freshwater and saltwater environments, allowing them to cover a wide range. They have been recorded swimming thousands of miles up rivers in search of new places to feed and breed.

Prefers nom-fiction books.
↓

No horns.
↓

Stronger bite force than a great white shark.
↓

350+ terrifying teeth!

*That was the sound of an Olympic swimmer being swallowed.

Electric eel.

~~Electrophorus.~~

Zapus shockus.

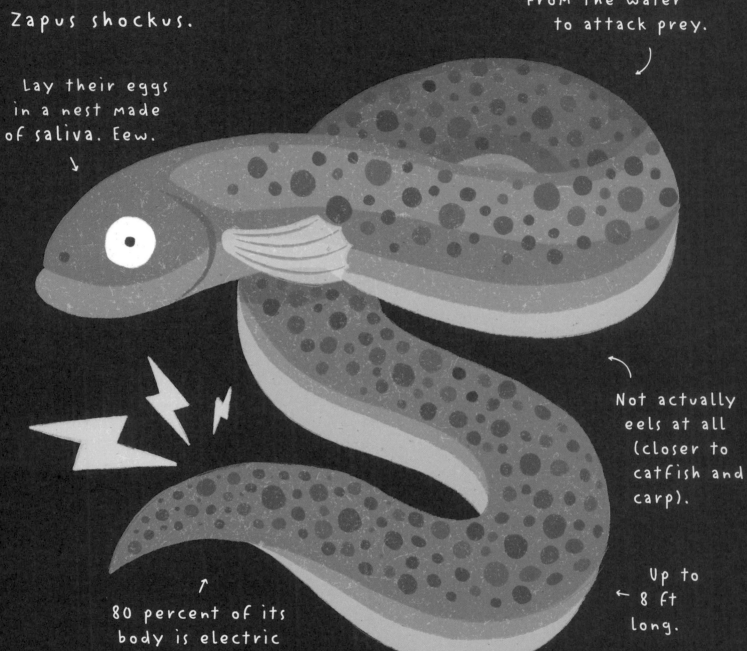

Known to lunge from the water to attack prey.

Lay their eggs in a nest made of saliva. Eew.

Not actually eels at all (closer to catfish and carp).

Up to 8 ft long.

80 percent of its body is electric organs!

These streamlined South American shockers come equipped with special organs capable of releasing electric charges of up to 860 volts (that's many times stronger than the electricity in your wall sockets)! All three species of electric eel use their superpowers for many purposes. Their charge is used to locate prey, a bit like radar. Once they come into contact with their lunch (usually smaller fish), the charge is used to stun it. And of course, electric eels use their powers to help keep potential predators at bay.

Hairy frog.

~~Trichobatrachus robustus.~~

Amphibious furreus.

Also known as "wolverine frog" and "horror frog."

Carnivorous croaker.

Known to kermit hideous crimes.

Hairy hopper.

Broken bones form "claws."

Red dermal papillae: the must-have accessory for frog dads this summer.

The most extraordinary thing about these frightful African amphibians isn't the "hair" around their hind legs—which is actually strands of skin—it is their "claws." As they mature, these frogs intentionally break their own finger bones, which then push through the skin to appear and function like claws! Hairy frogs are also known as "horror frogs," for obvious reasons. It is believed that the hairlike protrusions on their sides and hind legs allow brooding males to take in more oxygen while they look after their young.

Gila monster.

(Gila is pronounced HEE-luh.)

~~Heloderma suspectum.~~

Biteus goodnightus.

Spend about 95 percent of time underground.

A real little monster.

Tails can't fall off or regrow like most lizards.

They hibernate in winter. (Lazy.)

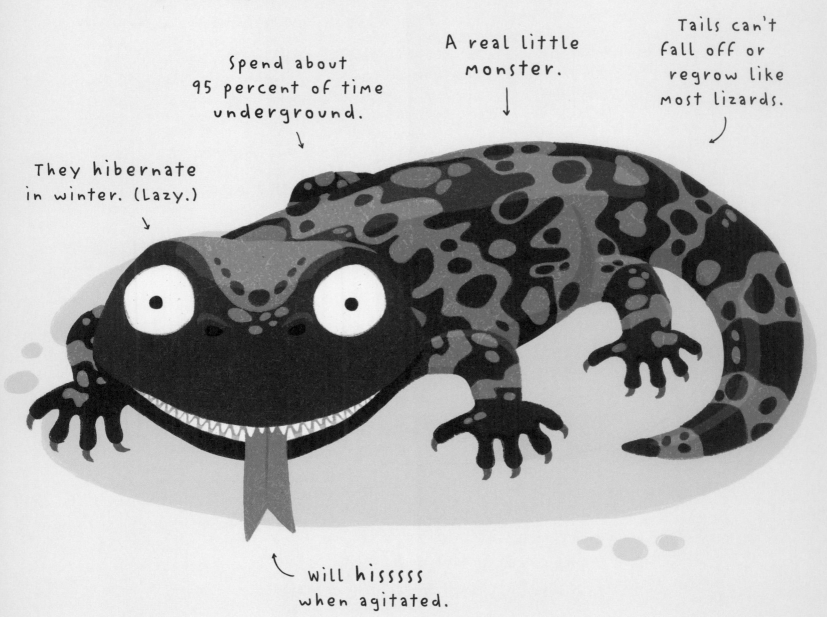

Will hisssss when agitated.

Dwelling in the deserts and rocky regions of Mexico and the southwestern United States, gilas are one of only a few venomous lizards on Earth. They take their name (the second part, at least) from the large, serrated teeth on their lower jaw. When they bite, venom seeps through these terrible teeth and into the unfortunate flesh of their victim. Once they've chomped, gilas will hold on, clamping down for as long as possible, giving enough time for the venom to take hold. Luckily for all around them, gilas only need to feed a few times each year, preying on eggs, birds, small mammals, and other lizards.

Cape buffalo.

~~Syncerus caffer.~~
Steerus clearus.

Always has the hump. ↙

Will charge without warning. Like a bank. ↙

Vicious vegan. ↘

Hide can be up to 2 in thick! ↙

Grumpy cow. ↘

Often butts heads with its neighbors. ↰

↑ Horrific horns.

While it is strictly vegetarian, the Cape buffalo is considered to be one of the most dangerous animals in Africa. Feared by all around them and capable of killing lions, these big beefy beasts are known to finish off more hunters than any other African animal. Weighing up to 1,750 lb, their size and typically grumpy behavior (they will often charge without warning!) make them a formidable force. Further, they typically hang out in herds of hundreds of individuals, so it's easy to see why some locals call these animals "the black death."

Spider-tailed horned viper.

~~Pseudocerastes urarachnoides.~~

Sssneakeus ssswindleus.

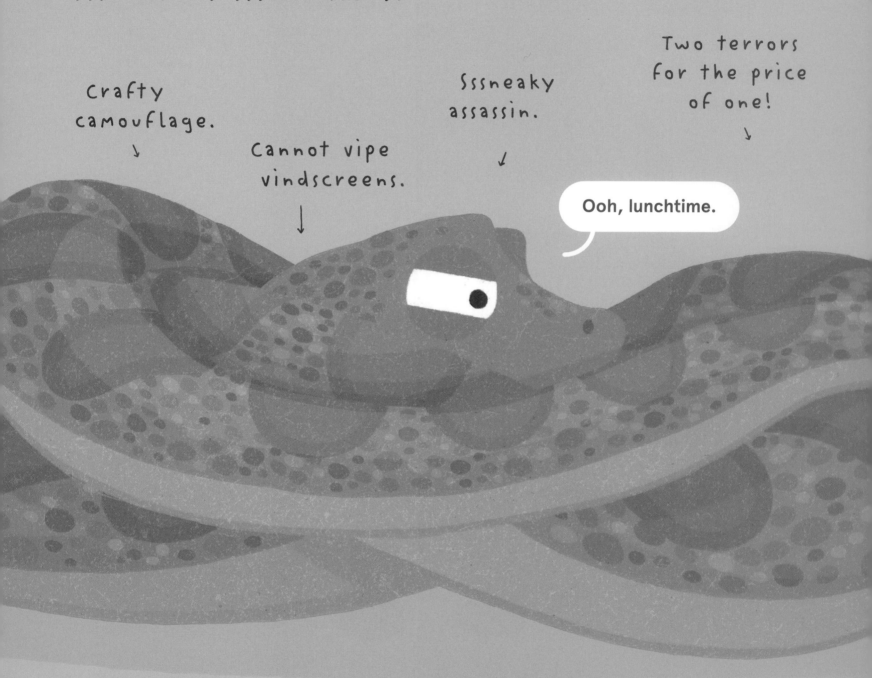

Crafty camouflage. ↓

Cannot vipe vindscreens. ↓

Sssneaky assassin. ↓

Two terrors for the price of one! ↓

Ooh, lunchtime.

The spider-tailed horned viper is a venomous snake from the Middle East. These ambush predators combine their camouflaged scales with a very special trick to catch their prey. Highly adapted scales at the tip of a viper's tail create an appendage that looks a lot like a spider. The appropriately named viper wiggles and jiggles this lure to help attract a feathered feed.

The viper hides in the sand and scrub as it wiggles its bait, mimicking the movements of a spider. When an unsuspecting bird pops in to peck at the "spider," the snake strikes at lightning speed (within 0.2 seconds) to snap up its lunch.

Soon-to-be an ex-sparrow.

Ooh, lunchtime.

Monstrous mimicry.

Atrocious appendage. →

The birds are so focused on their own lunch that they don't notice the viper until it's too late. However, studies have shown that only migratory (visiting) birds fall prey to the treacherous tactics of the spider-tailed horned viper. This suggests that the local population have figured out the snake's tricks, and stay well clear (no matter how delicious that spider might appear).

Common vampire bat.

~~Desmodus rotundus.~~

Vladus battus.

Favorite ice-cream flavor? Vein-illa. ↓

Can be a real pain in the neck. ↓

Creepy little thumbs. ⌒

↑ Leathery wings. Eew.

← Always looking for their necks victim.

Vampire bats have fewer teeth than any other species of bat—and for good reason. They are the only mammals known to survive solely on a diet of blood! Each night, these nocturnal nibblers drink about half their body weight of the red stuff, from prey such as cows, pigs, and horses. Unlike vampires in fiction, they do not suck blood, but make a small cut in the skin of their victim and lap it up. Because of their nutrient-poor diet, bats that can't find blood for two nights in a row will typically die. Fortunately, roostmates will often help out unlucky bats, by regurgitating (vomiting) blood for them to drink.

Spotted hyena.

Crocuta crocuta.

Chucklus chucklus.

You will never meet a lowena.

Dress sense: spotty at best.

Sense of humor: wild.

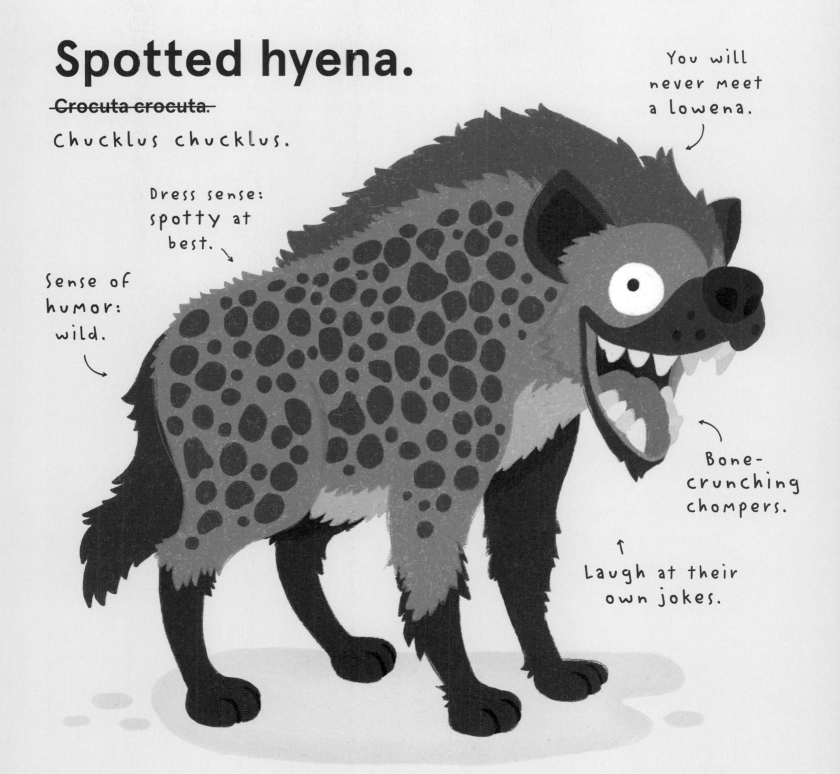

Bone-crunching chompers.

Laugh at their own jokes.

Spotted hyenas are often called laughing hyenas, as they communicate through complex sequences of yelps, cackles, titters, and whoops! However, hyenas are no joke. These highly intelligent predators live in complex social groups and are capable of taking down huge prey such as antelope, zebras, and even wildebeest. Their female-led clans can reach well over 50 members, each packing a big brain and jaws capable of crunching through the bones of any of those big herbivores. This ability allows hyenas to get to the nutrient-rich marrow inside bones, which is not available to most other predators.

Goliath birdeater.

~~Theraphosa blondi.~~
Massivus haireum.

The world's heaviest spider spans about the width of a dinner plate and weighs in at around 6 oz (impressive for an arachnid!). Delivering venom comparable to a wasp sting through its fangs, the goliath birdeater has another trick up its many sleeves. Its body is covered in detachable barbed hairs that stick in the skin and eyes of any potential predator, causing great irritation for days, which can lead to possible infection.

Dwelling in burrows in the rainforests of northern South America, birdeaters hunt by night, sensing vibrations in the ground before pouncing on their prey and injecting their venom.

Terrible eyesight.

Spiders can't eat solids, so they liquefy their lunch, then suck it up. Yummy.

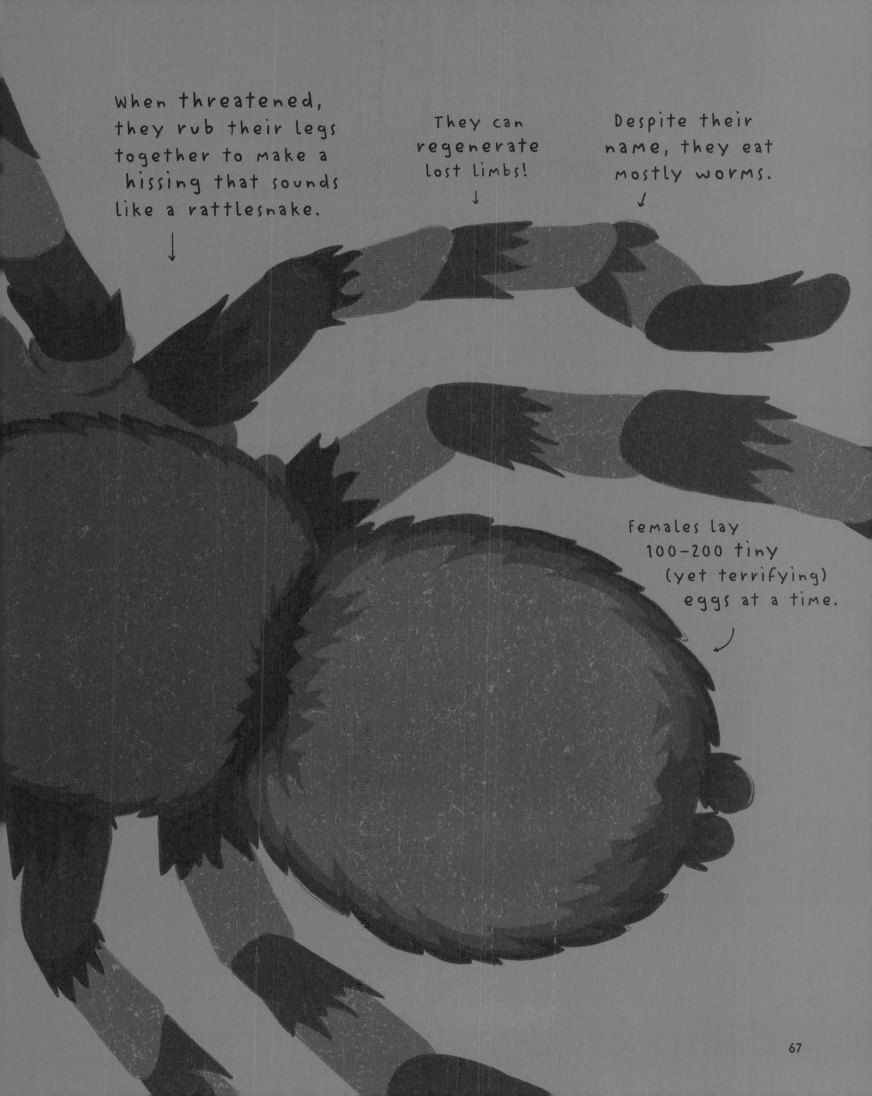

When threatened, they rub their legs together to make a hissing that sounds like a rattlesnake.
↓

They can regenerate lost limbs!
↓

Despite their name, they eat mostly worms.
↙

Females lay 100–200 tiny (yet terrifying) eggs at a time.
↙

Great horned owl.

Bubo virginianus.

Hornus hootus.

Silent but deadly.

Not really horns (just feathery tufts).

Tufts stand up when interested and fall flat when irritated.

Short, wide wings allow them to zigzag through the forest.

Can swivel their heads more than 270°. Creepy!

Can fly at 40 mi per hour!

Nocturnal nightmare.

Bone-crunching talons.

Great horned owls are big, aggressive, powerful birds of prey with talons strong enough to crack the bones and spines of even large animals. Their preferred fare includes, well, whatever is unlucky enough to pass by their perch—from frogs to foxes, skunks to scorpions. These big birds can hear a meal from up to 10 mi away, and their eyes are around 35 times more sensitive than ours. Combine these traits with their ability to fly *almost* silently, and it's no wonder that these owls are such successful predators.

Bull ant.

~~Myrmecia gulosa.~~

Chompus stingus.

Serious stinger.
↓

Ouch!

90 species of bull ant in Australia.

Some bull ants can jump over 2 in (in your direction). Argh!
↓

Massive mandibles.
↓

Can carry seven times their own body weight!

Unlike other ants, their eyesight is excellent.

Ants branched off from their waspy ancestors over 140 million years ago, yet bull ants make the link very clear. With their wasplike bodies, this ancient group of ants don't communicate through scent, and they live in far smaller colonies. But what they lack in social skills, they make up for in aggression! At up to 1.5 in long, bull ants are the largest and most hostile species of ant on Earth. They use their huge mandibles (jaws) to chomp onto anything that comes near their nest, before repeatedly injecting venom with the stinger at the end of their abdomen. These incredibly painful stings can hurt the poor victim for days, and can even be fatal to humans.

Portuguese man o' war.

~~Physalia physalis.~~

Colonious atrocious.

These fantastic floaters are easily mistaken for jellyfish. However, the Portuguese man o' war is actually a colony of teeny-tiny animals (called zooids) that work together to form the main parts of the organism. There are four kinds of zooid, each with its own role to play in support of the mother ship.

Meet the Zooids...

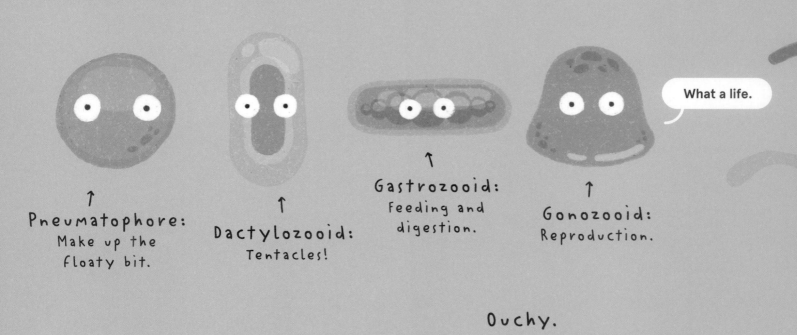

↑
Pneumatophore:
Make up the
floaty bit.

↑
Dactylozooid:
Tentacles!

↑
Gastrozooid:
Feeding and
digestion.

↑
Gonozooid:
Reproduction.

What a life.

Ouchy.
↓

↑
Ouchy.

↗
Train of
pain.

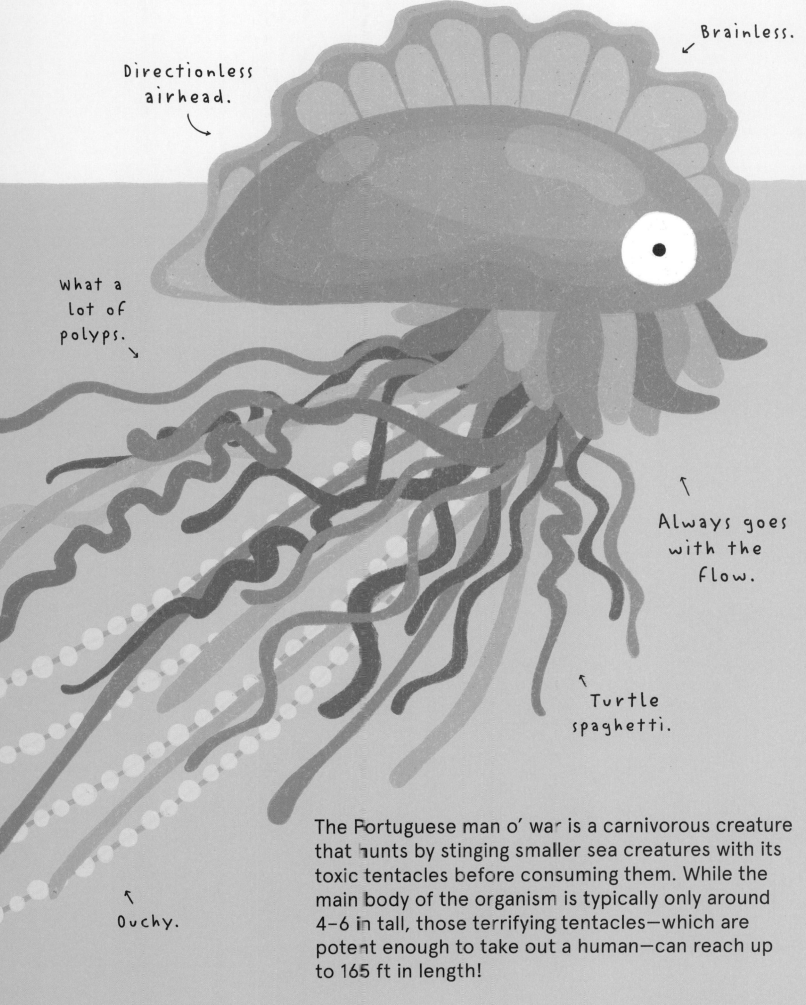

Brainless.

Directionless airhead.

What a lot of polyps.

Always goes with the flow.

Turtle spaghetti.

Ouchy.

The Portuguese man o' war is a carnivorous creature that hunts by stinging smaller sea creatures with its toxic tentacles before consuming them. While the main body of the organism is typically only around 4–6 in tall, those terrifying tentacles—which are potent enough to take out a human—can reach up to 165 ft in length!

Wolverine.

~~Gulo gulo.~~

Gluttonus gobblea.

Stinky coat.

Look out below! Drops from trees!

Big dog? Tiny bear? No! Massive weasel!

Musky butt.

Bone-crunching teeth and jaws.

Claws out (always!).

Contrary to their common name, wolverines are not closely related to dogs—they are the largest, most ferocious member of the weasel family. These carnivores roam huge territories in search of prey such as rabbits, mice, and gophers, using their thick waterproof coat to keep out the cold. As ambush predators, they hide out in trees or bushes before pouncing on their prey, deploying those massive nonretractable claws. Wolverines also scavenge the prey of much larger animals, and are known to scare even grizzly bears away from their kill, through aggressive behavior, including growls and hisses.

Goliath tigerfish.

~~Hydrocynus goliath.~~

Tootheus giganticus.

This fish will turn you into chips. ↓

One chomp can cut their victim in half. ↓

All ponds are too small for this big fish. ↷

The heaviest on record weighed a whopping 154 lb! ↑

A dentist's nightmare. ↑

These West African river monsters reach lengths of up to 5 ft, with a mouth full of razor-sharp teeth measuring a shark-sized 1 in! Goliath tigerfish hunt in calmer stretches of rivers and lakes, typically lying in wait to ambush their prey. When they strike, they chomp down with such force that the bite often literally cuts their prey in half. Once they kill their prey, they don't worry about chewing and just swallow their meals whole. While they prefer the taste of other fish, goliath tigerfish have been known to attack crocodiles, humans, and even snag unsuspecting birds from the air.

Whistling kite.

~~Haliastur sphenurus.~~

Predatorius prometheus.

Avian arsonist.
↓

Feathered Firestarter.

↑
Step 1:
Plumed pyromaniac
picks burning stick
from bushfire.

The whistling kite is one of three Australian birds of prey known locally as firehawks. Along with black kites and brown falcons, whistling kites use fire to hunt. Firehawks cannot start fires from scratch, but they intentionally spread them by picking up burning branches from existing fires and dropping them on the scrubby homes of unsuspecting small mammals, lizards, and insects.

Once the burning stick is dropped onto the bush, the residents have a choice to make—either stay put and risk getting toasted in the fire, or flee and try to avoid being snapped up by the circling firehawks.

↑
Step 2:
Fire stick dropped on unburned bush.

↑
Step 3:
Small mammals scatter from burning bush.

Step 4:
← Rattus rattus, medium-rare.

Ah, rats.

Of course, the new fires cause the mammals, lizards, and insects to evacuate. At this point they become easy prey for the raptors.

Bluespotted ribbontail ray.

~~Taeniura lymma.~~

Spottus stingus.

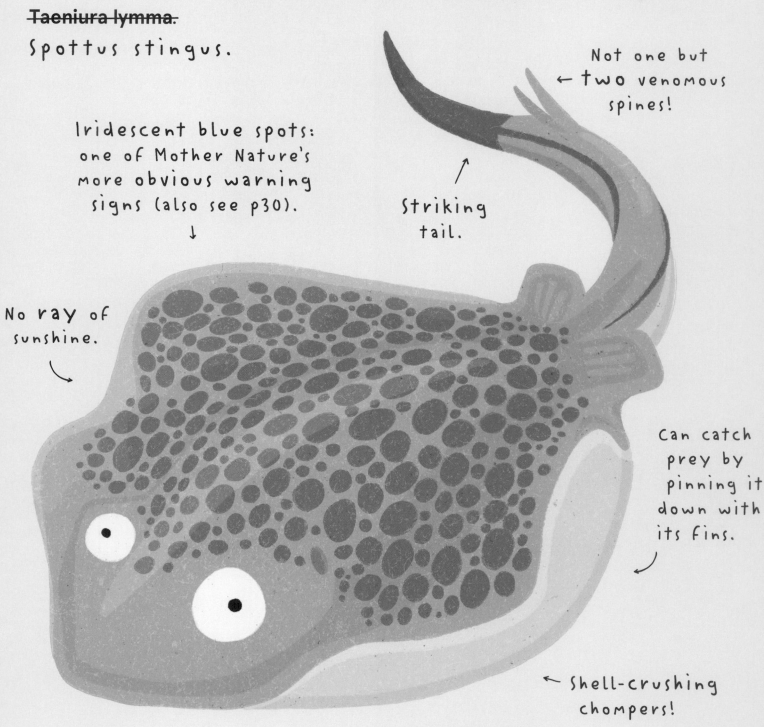

Iridescent blue spots:
one of Mother Nature's
more obvious warning
signs (also see p30).
↓

Striking
tail.
↑

Not one but
← two venomous
spines!

No ray of
sunshine.

Can catch
prey by
pinning it
down with
its fins.

← Shell-crushing
chompers!

Lurking in the warm, shallow sands of the Indian and western Pacific Oceans, these rad rays can whip their spined tails to inject a venom which can be fatal to most forms of life (you and me included). However, the bluespotted ribbontail ray will only lash out like this when threatened. Their preferred mode of operation is to nestle into the seafloor and forage for their fodder (crustaceans, worms, and molluscs, preferably).

African lion.

~~Panthera leo.~~

Lionel richii.

King of the ~~jungle~~ savanna.

Spends most of the day (up to 20 hours) sleeping or snoozing.

Hello ...

Females do most of the hunting. Yet the adult males eat first. Rude.

The circle of life ends right here.

Can munch 88 lb of meat in a single meal. Greedy.

Can run at up to 50 mi per hour (in short bursts).

While lionesses do up to 95 percent of the hunting, male African lions tend to stay home to "guard the fort." Nevertheless, the adult males seem to get the lion's share of our attention. Male lions' magnificent manes grow darker as they age, and signal their animal's rank within the family group (a.k.a. pride). A pride of lions dominates the food chain in their savanna home, each munching their way through up to 88 lb of—deep breath—warthogs, buffaloes, hares, mice, antelopes, wild dogs, other cats, birds, turtles, lizards, crocodiles, young elephants, rhinos, hippos, giraffes...in a single sitting!

In closing.

A great man once said, "The only thing we have to fear is fear itself"...just before he was eaten by a bear. If we learn only one thing from the animals in this book, it might be that sometimes, fear is there for a reason. The creatures that provoke fear in our minds help to connect us to the instincts passed on from our ancestors, who lived alongside some *really* fearsome animals.

These instincts guide us toward some things, and cause us to fear others. But just because we fear them, it doesn't make the animals in this book bad—they are just doing the things they need to do to survive, thrive, and make babies. And just like the animals in this book, it is worth remembering that we can all be a little ~~bit fearsome~~ atrocious, from time to time.

Index.

↑
Unbearable.

Sssneaky.

Steer
clear.

Will turn
you into
chips.

↓

Footlong
frightener.